FR. PETER AMBROSE

Our Lady of Lourdes Novena

Copyright © 2025 by Fr. Peter Ambrose

All rights reserved. No part of this publication may be reproduced, stored or transmitted in any form or by any means, electronic, mechanical, photocopying, recording, scanning, or otherwise without written permission from the publisher. It is illegal to copy this book, post it to a website, or distribute it by any other means without permission.

First edition

This book was professionally typeset on Reedsy.
Find out more at reedsy.com

Contents

Table of Contents	1
Introduction	2
How to Pray the Novena	4
Day 1: The Call to Faith	7
Day 2: The Healing Power of Lourdes	9
Day 3: The Humility of St. Bernadette	11
Day 4: Mary, Refuge of Sinners	13
Day 5: The Immaculate Conception	14
Day 6: Trusting in Divine Providence	15
Day 7: Consolation for the Afflicted	16
Day 8: The Waters of Lourdes – A Fountain of Grace	18
Day 9: Our Lady of Lourdes, Patroness of Miracles	20
Litany of Our Lady of Lourdes	22
Conclusion	24

Table of Contents

Introduction
    How to Pray the Novena
    Day 1: The Call to Faith
Day 2: The Healing Power of Lourdes
Day 3: The Humility of St. Bernadette
Day 4: Mary, Refuge of Sinners
Day 5: The Immaculate Conception
Day 6: Trusting in Divine Providence
Day 7: Consolation for the Afflicted
Day 8: The Waters of Lourdes – A Fountain of Grace
Day 9: Our Lady of Lourdes, Patroness of Miracles
Litany of Our Lady of Lourdes
Prayer of Consecration to Our Lady of Lourdes
Conclusion

Introduction

The Significance of Our Lady of Lourdes

Our Lady of Lourdes is one of the most beloved Marian apparitions in the Catholic Church. Her appearance to St. Bernadette Soubirous in 1858 in Lourdes, France, transformed the small village into a center of faith, healing, and devotion. Lourdes has since become one of the most visited pilgrimage sites in the world, drawing millions of faithful each year who seek physical and spiritual healing. The Blessed Virgin's message at Lourdes emphasizes prayer, repentance, and trust in God's mercy, offering hope to all who turn to her in faith. Through her maternal intercession, Our Lady continues to guide believers toward her Son, Jesus Christ, bringing peace and comfort to those in need.

The Apparitions to St. Bernadette

On February 11, 1858, fourteen-year-old Bernadette Soubirous experienced the first of eighteen apparitions of the Blessed Virgin Mary at the grotto of Massabielle. Describing the vision as a "beautiful lady" dressed in white with a blue sash, Bernadette was instructed to pray and return to the grotto. Over the course of the apparitions, Our Lady revealed herself as the "Immaculate Conception" and called for prayer, penance, and devotion. Despite skepticism from civil and religious authorities, Bernadette remained steadfast in recounting her visions. The miraculous spring that emerged from the grotto at Our Lady's direction continues to flow today, with many pilgrims attributing healings and graces to its waters.

Messages and Miracles of Lourdes

The central messages of Lourdes revolve around faith, repentance, and healing. Our Lady called for sinners to turn back to God, urging them to pray and offer sacrifices for the conversion of souls. She also encouraged devotion to the Rosary, emphasizing the power of prayer in drawing closer to Christ. One of the most enduring miracles of Lourdes is the healing spring, which has been the source of numerous documented miracles. The Catholic Church has officially recognized several miraculous healings attributed to Lourdes, reinforcing its status as a sacred place of grace. The countless testimonies of those who have experienced spiritual renewal and healing serve as a testament to Our Lady's ongoing presence and intercession.

The Power of Marian Devotion

Devotion to Our Lady of Lourdes deepens one's relationship with Christ, as Mary always leads the faithful to her Son. Through prayers, novenas, and acts of faith, believers entrust their needs and sufferings to her compassionate care. Lourdes serves as a reminder that Mary continues to intercede for humanity, offering comfort, healing, and guidance. By meditating on her messages and seeking her intercession, we grow in holiness and draw closer to the heart of Jesus. In praying this novena, we unite ourselves with countless others who have turned to Our Lady of Lourdes in faith, trusting in her motherly love and powerful intercession.

How to Pray the Novena

Praying a novena is a beautiful way to deepen your devotion and seek the intercession of Our Lady of Lourdes. This nine-day prayer journey allows us to reflect on Mary's messages at Lourdes and to bring our needs before God with confidence. Whether you are praying for healing, conversion, or a special grace, this novena is an opportunity to grow in faith and trust in God's mercy.

Structure of the Novena

A novena traditionally consists of a specific prayer or set of prayers repeated for nine consecutive days. The *Our Lady of Lourdes Novena* follows this structure:

1. **Opening Prayer** – A short invocation to Our Lady of Lourdes, asking for her intercession.
2. **Daily Reflection** – A meditation on themes related to the Lourdes apparitions, such as faith, humility, healing, or conversion.
3. **Novena Prayer** – A special prayer addressed to Our Lady of Lourdes, seeking her guidance and grace.
4. **Personal Intentions** – A moment of silent prayer to present your personal needs and petitions.
5. **Closing Prayer** – Ending with a Marian prayer, such as the *Hail Mary, Memorare,* or *Litany of Our Lady of Lourdes*.

You may also choose to pray this novena alone, with family, or as part of a group devotion.

Suggested Intentions

While you can pray this novena for any intention, common requests include:

- **Healing** – Physical, emotional, or spiritual healing for yourself or a loved one.
- **Faith and Trust** – Strengthening your faith and deepening your trust in God's will.
- **Conversion and Repentance** – Seeking the grace to turn away from sin and grow in holiness.
- **Peace and Strength** – Asking for courage and peace in times of suffering or difficulty.
- **For the Sick and Suffering** – Interceding for those in hospitals, facing chronic illness, or struggling with mental health.
- **For the Church and the World** – Praying for the needs of the Church, for an increase in vocations, and for peace in the world.

You may focus on one specific intention throughout the novena or bring different requests each day.

Incorporating the Rosary and Other Prayers

The Rosary is a powerful way to enhance your novena. Our Lady at Lourdes encouraged prayer, particularly the Rosary, which St. Bernadette often prayed during the apparitions. You may choose to:

- Pray a full **Rosary** (all five decades) before or after the novena prayer.
- Pray one decade of the Rosary, meditating on a mystery related to the day's reflection.
- Add Marian prayers such as the **Memorare, Angelus, or Litany of Our Lady of Lourdes**.
- Conclude with a **prayer of consecration** to Our Lady of Lourdes, entrusting yourself to her care.

By praying this novena with devotion, we open ourselves to the graces Our Lady of Lourdes desires to bring into our lives, trusting in her powerful intercession and the infinite love of God.

Day 1: The Call to Faith

Reflection: Trusting in God's Plan

Faith is the foundation of our relationship with God. When Our Lady appeared to St. Bernadette at Lourdes, she did not choose someone powerful or influential but a humble and illiterate girl from a poor family. Bernadette did not fully understand why she was chosen, yet she trusted in God's plan and remained obedient to Mary's instructions, despite skepticism and opposition.

In our own lives, we may struggle to trust in God, especially when faced with uncertainty, suffering, or unanswered prayers. However, just as Mary guided Bernadette, she also invites us to trust that God is leading us, even when we cannot see the full picture. True faith is not about having all the answers but about surrendering to God's will with confidence, knowing that He works all things for our good.

Let us reflect today: Do I trust in God's plan, even when life is difficult? Do I turn to Mary for guidance and intercession when my faith feels weak?

Prayer for Strength in Faith

Heavenly Father, I thank You for the gift of faith. In times of doubt and difficulty, help me to trust in Your divine plan, just as St. Bernadette trusted in You at Lourdes. Through the intercession of Our Lady of Lourdes, strengthen my faith so that I may follow You with confidence and peace. Let my heart be open to Your will, and may I

always seek Your presence in my life. Amen.
   (Pray the Hail Mary, Our Father, and Glory Be.)

Day 2: The Healing Power of Lourdes

Reflection: Seeking Physical and Spiritual Healing
One of the greatest miracles of Lourdes is the healing power that flows from its waters. Since the time of the apparitions, thousands of people have experienced physical and spiritual healing at the grotto. Some have been cured of incurable illnesses, while others have found peace, strength, and renewal in their faith.

Healing comes in many forms—sometimes God grants physical healing, but often He gives us the grace to endure suffering with patience and hope. Our Lady of Lourdes reminds us that God's love is greater than our pain, and when we place our burdens in His hands, He transforms them into opportunities for grace. Whether we seek healing for ourselves or others, we can trust that Mary, our Mother, intercedes for us with great compassion.

Let us reflect today: Do I bring my sufferings to Jesus with trust, or do I hold onto fear and despair? Do I pray for those who are sick and suffering, asking Our Lady of Lourdes to intercede for them?

Prayer for the Sick and Suffering
Loving Mother, Our Lady of Lourdes, you appeared to St. Bernadette as a sign of hope and healing. I come before you today, seeking your intercession for all who are sick and suffering. If it is God's will, may those in need experience physical healing, but above all, may they find peace, strength, and trust in His mercy. Help me to accept my own sufferings with faith, knowing that God's grace is always sufficient.

Amen.

(*Pray the Hail Mary, Our Father, and Glory Be.*)

Day 3: The Humility of St. Bernadette

Reflection: Embracing Humility in Our Lives

St. Bernadette Soubirous was chosen by Our Lady, not because of her intelligence, status, or abilities, but because of her humility. She did not seek attention or glory; instead, she accepted her role as Mary's messenger with simplicity and obedience. Despite facing disbelief, ridicule, and suffering, she remained steadfast, saying, *"I was asked to tell you, not to make you believe."*

True humility is not about thinking less of ourselves but about recognizing that everything we have is a gift from God. It allows us to accept our weaknesses and trust in God's strength. In a world that often values pride, success, and recognition, Bernadette's example reminds us that God looks at the heart.

Let us reflect today: Do I seek recognition and approval from others, or do I live with humility, trusting in God's plan? Am I willing to serve others without expecting praise?

Prayer for a Humble Heart

Dear Lord, You lift up the humble and fill the lowly with Your grace. Through the intercession of St. Bernadette, help me to embrace humility in my life. Teach me to serve others selflessly, to accept my weaknesses with trust in You, and to seek only Your will. May my heart be small, so that You may be great within me. Amen.

(Pray the Hail Mary, Our Father, and Glory Be.)

Day 4: Mary, Refuge of Sinners

Reflection: Turning Back to God's Mercy

At Lourdes, Our Lady called for prayer and penance, reminding us of the need for conversion. She appeared not to condemn but to invite all sinners to return to God's mercy. The grotto of Lourdes has become a place of reconciliation, where countless souls have rediscovered the love and forgiveness of Christ.

No sin is too great for God's mercy. Mary, as our loving Mother, intercedes for us and gently leads us back to her Son. Just as she called St. Bernadette to prayer and sacrifice for sinners, she calls each of us to repentance. Whether we have wandered far from God or struggle with daily faults, we are invited to turn to Him with a sincere heart.

Let us reflect today: Do I acknowledge my sins and seek God's mercy regularly? Do I pray for the conversion of others, trusting in the power of God's grace?

Prayer for Repentance and Conversion

O Mary, Refuge of Sinners, you never turn away those who seek your help. Pray for me, that I may have the courage to recognize my sins and seek God's mercy with a contrite heart. Lead me to the sacrament of confession, where I may receive the grace of forgiveness. Help all those who are far from God to return to Him, so that we may one day rejoice together in His presence. Amen.

(Pray the Hail Mary, Our Father, and Glory Be.)

Day 5: The Immaculate Conception

Reflection: Understanding Mary's Purity and Role in Salvation
When Our Lady appeared to St. Bernadette, she identified herself with the words, *"I am the Immaculate Conception."* This declaration affirmed the Church's teaching that Mary was conceived without original sin, a singular grace granted to her in preparation for her role as the Mother of God.

Mary's purity is not only physical but also spiritual—her heart was entirely devoted to God, free from sin and completely obedient to His will. As the Immaculate Conception, she is the perfect model of holiness, inviting us to strive for purity in our own lives. Through her intercession, we can ask for the grace to reject sin and grow in love for God.

Let us reflect today: Do I seek to imitate Mary's purity in my thoughts, words, and actions? Do I turn to her as my model in the spiritual life?

Prayer for Purity of Heart
O Immaculate Virgin Mary, you were preserved from sin from the moment of your conception, and your heart remained pure and holy before God. Through your intercession, help me to strive for purity in my own life, that I may love God with all my heart and soul. Protect me from temptation, strengthen me in virtue, and lead me ever closer to your Son, Jesus Christ. Amen.

(Pray the Hail Mary, Our Father, and Glory Be.)

Day 6: Trusting in Divine Providence

Reflection: Surrendering to God's Will

At Lourdes, Our Lady's message was one of trust and surrender. St. Bernadette was asked to deliver messages that she did not always understand, yet she remained faithful, knowing that God's plan was greater than her own understanding.

Trusting in Divine Providence means believing that God is in control, even when life seems uncertain or difficult. It requires us to surrender our fears, worries, and desires to Him, knowing that He loves us and works all things for our good. When we entrust our lives to God, we experience true peace, just as Mary did when she said, *"Let it be done to me according to your word."*

Let us reflect today: Do I trust in God's plan for my life, even when I do not understand it? Am I willing to surrender my worries to Him, believing that He will take care of me?

Prayer for Trust and Confidence in God

Heavenly Father, You hold all things in Your hands, and nothing happens outside of Your loving will. Through the intercession of Our Lady of Lourdes, help me to trust in Your divine plan. Give me the grace to surrender my fears, knowing that You are my refuge and strength. May I follow You with confidence and peace, trusting that You are always with me. Amen.

(Pray the Hail Mary, Our Father, and Glory Be.)

Day 7: Consolation for the Afflicted

Reflection: Finding Hope in Our Lady's Comfort
Throughout history, Mary has been a source of comfort for those who suffer. At Lourdes, she appeared to St. Bernadette with a message of hope, offering reassurance to those burdened by illness, sorrow, and despair. The grotto at Lourdes has become a place where countless pilgrims find peace, healing, and renewed strength in God's love.

Suffering is an unavoidable part of life, but we are never alone in our struggles. Mary, our Mother, walks with us, just as she stood at the foot of the Cross with her Son. She understands our pain and offers her maternal love to console us. When we turn to her, she gently leads us to Jesus, the source of true healing and peace.

Let us reflect today: Do I turn to Our Lady in times of sorrow, trusting in her comfort? Do I bring the hope of Christ to those who are suffering around me?

Prayer for Those in Sorrow and Despair
O Mary, Mother of Consolation, you comfort all who suffer and weep. I bring before you all those who are burdened by sorrow, pain, or despair. Be their refuge and strength, and remind them that they are not alone. Through your intercession, may they find hope in God's love and trust in His divine plan. Help me to bring comfort to others through kindness, prayer, and faith. Amen.

DAY 7: CONSOLATION FOR THE AFFLICTED

(Pray the Hail Mary, Our Father, and Glory Be.)

Day 8: The Waters of Lourdes – A Fountain of Grace

Reflection: The Symbolism of Water in Our Faith

One of the most remarkable aspects of Lourdes is its miraculous spring, discovered by St. Bernadette at the request of Our Lady. Over the years, these waters have become a powerful sign of healing and renewal, with many experiencing physical cures and spiritual conversions after drinking or bathing in them.

Water has deep symbolism in our faith. In Baptism, we are cleansed of original sin and made new in Christ. In the Gospels, Jesus speaks of Himself as the *living water* that quenches our deepest thirst. The waters of Lourdes remind us that God's grace is ever-flowing, ready to cleanse, heal, and refresh our souls.

Let us reflect today: Do I seek God's grace to renew my heart? Do I approach the sacraments, especially Baptism and Confession, as true fountains of divine mercy?

Prayer for Renewal and Grace

Heavenly Father, You have given us the gift of water as a sign of Your life-giving grace. Through the intercession of Our Lady of Lourdes, may I be renewed in spirit, cleansed of sin, and strengthened in faith. Pour out Your healing grace upon me,

DAY 8: THE WATERS OF LOURDES – A FOUNTAIN OF GRACE

that I may grow closer to You each day. Help me to trust in Your mercy and be an instrument of Your love to others. Amen.

(Pray the Hail Mary, Our Father, and Glory Be.)

Day 9: Our Lady of Lourdes, Patroness of Miracles

Reflection: Seeking Our Lady's Intercession with Confidence
Our Lady of Lourdes is known as the *Patroness of Miracles*, a title earned through the countless healings and conversions attributed to her intercession. From the miraculous cures at the grotto to the unseen graces received by those who seek her, Mary continues to be a loving mother who hears and answers the prayers of her children.

While miracles are extraordinary signs of God's power, the greatest miracle is the transformation of our hearts. Through Mary, we are invited to trust more deeply in God's providence, to believe that nothing is impossible for Him, and to surrender our needs with faith. When we approach Our Lady with confidence, she carries our petitions to her Son, who always listens with love.

Let us reflect today: Do I believe in God's power to work miracles in my life? Do I trust that Our Lady intercedes for me, even when I do not see immediate answers?

Prayer for Miraculous Help
O Mary, Patroness of Miracles, you appeared at Lourdes as a sign of God's mercy and love. I come before you today with faith, seeking your powerful intercession.

DAY 9: OUR LADY OF LOURDES, PATRONESS OF MIRACLES

If it be God's will, grant me the miracle I seek (mention your request). But above all, help me to trust in His divine plan, knowing that He always provides what is best for me. Strengthen my faith, fill my heart with hope, and lead me ever closer to Jesus. Amen.

(*Pray the Hail Mary, Our Father, and Glory Be.*)

Litany of Our Lady of Lourdes

Lord, have mercy on us.
    Christ, have mercy on us.
    Lord, have mercy on us.
Christ, hear us.
Christ, graciously hear us.
God the Father of Heaven, *have mercy on us.*
God the Son, Redeemer of the world, *have mercy on us.*
God the Holy Spirit, *have mercy on us.*
Holy Trinity, One God, *have mercy on us.*
Holy Mary, Mother of God, *pray for us.*
Our Lady of Lourdes, *pray for us.*
Our Lady, Immaculate Conception, *pray for us.*
Our Lady, shining with purity, *pray for us.*
Our Lady, Mother of the Church, *pray for us.*
Our Lady, refuge of sinners, *pray for us.*
Our Lady, comforter of the afflicted, *pray for us.*
Our Lady, health of the sick, *pray for us.*
Our Lady, fountain of grace, *pray for us.*
Our Lady of Lourdes, healer of the weak, *pray for us.*
Our Lady of Lourdes, hope of the suffering, *pray for us.*
Our Lady of Lourdes, intercessor for miracles, *pray for us.*

Lamb of God, who takes away the sins of the world, *spare us, O Lord.*

Lamb of God, who takes away the sins of the world, *graciously hear us, O Lord.*

Lamb of God, who takes away the sins of the world, *have mercy on us.*

V. Pray for us, O Holy Mother of God.

R. That we may be made worthy of the promises of Christ.

Let us pray:

O God, who by the Immaculate Conception of the Blessed Virgin Mary prepared a worthy dwelling for Your Son, grant, we beseech You, that through the intercession of Our Lady of Lourdes, we may be healed in body and soul and be led to the joys of eternal life. Through Christ our Lord. *Amen.*

Prayer of Consecration to Our Lady of Lourdes

O Mary, Our Lady of Lourdes,
I consecrate myself to you today and forever.
I give you my heart, my soul, and my whole being,
that I may be united with your Immaculate Heart.
O Mother most pure,
lead me ever closer to your Son, Jesus Christ.
Teach me to trust in His love,
to embrace His will,
and to seek His mercy at all times.
Our Lady of Lourdes,
patroness of the sick and suffering,
intercede for me and for all who call upon you.
Strengthen my faith,
renew my hope,
and help me to live in the light of Christ's grace.
I place myself under your protection,
now and always,
that I may one day share in the glory of Heaven.
Amen.

Conclusion

Living Out the Message of Lourdes in Daily Life

The message of Our Lady of Lourdes is not just for those who travel to the grotto in France—it is a call to all of us, wherever we are. Mary's words to St. Bernadette encourage us to live with faith, humility, prayer, and trust in God's mercy.

As we conclude this novena, let us reflect on how we can carry the spirit of Lourdes into our daily lives. We can deepen our faith through prayer, frequent the sacraments, especially Confession and the Eucharist, and show compassion to the sick and suffering. Like Bernadette, we are called to trust in God's will and to live with simplicity and love.

May this novena inspire us to draw closer to Our Lady, seeking her guidance and intercession in all that we do. Just as the healing waters of Lourdes continue to bring grace to pilgrims, may our hearts be filled with the living water of Christ, refreshing us with His peace and strength.

Let us go forth with renewed faith, carrying the message of Lourdes in our hearts, and sharing it with others through our love and witness.

Final Blessing and Encouragement

Heavenly Father, we thank You for the graces received through this novena. May the prayers we have offered bear fruit in our lives, drawing us closer to You and to Our Lady. Help us to live out the message of Lourdes each day, trusting in Your mercy and sharing Your love with the world. Through the intercession of Our Lady of Lourdes, bless us and keep us always in Your care. Amen.

Our Lady of Lourdes, pray for us!
St. Bernadette, pray for us!

(Pray the Hail Mary, Our Father, and Glory Be.)

Made in the USA
Monee, IL
25 September 2025